Successful
Fiber Optic
Installation-
A Rapid Start Guide

Eric R. Pearson, CFOS
President
Pearson Technologies Inc.
4671 Hickory Bend Drive
Acworth, GA 30102

fiberguru@ptnowire.com
770-490-9991

www.ptnowire.com

deliberately blank

Table of Contents

1   Introduction

The objective of this Rapid Start Guide [RSG] is to 'jump start you' on your path to becoming successful in fiber optic installation. This RSG will 'jump start' you by providing two types of information. The first type is the basic information the installer must have to get started in fiber optic installation. Without this information, the installer will have little chance of achieving the three goals of installation. These goals are:

> Low power loss
>
> Low installation cost
>
> High reliability

The second type of information is the more subtle information that the installer must have to be consistently successful as a professional installer. In addition, this subtle information enables the installer to troubleshoot problems.

As this is a Rapid Start Guide (RSG), it will provide the first type and a list of the information in the second type. See 'Other Terms' for a list of this subtle, but essential information.

In addition, this RSG will provide references to sources of information on the second type. Those references will be to chapters in <u>Professional Fiber Optic Installation- The Essentials</u> (ISBN 978-0976975434). This comprehensive, 342-page, field installation reference and training text is available from Pearson Technologies Inc.

One final note: this Guide will reference the Building Wiring Standard, TIA/EIA-568-C, which is the latest version of the document used by most data network designers to design and implement their data networks.

2   Networks

2.1   Key Terms

Optoelectronics, transceivers, link, segment, connection, connectors, splices, full duplex, backbone

2.2   Overview

From the perspective of the installer, a fiber optic network consists of the complete optical signal path between two electronic devices. The electronic devices can be any device that converts an electrical signal to an optical signal or the reverse. Because of this conversion, we call these devices optoelectronics. Such devices can be:

Switches

Routers

Fiber optic NICs

Media converters

GBICs

Since most fiber optic optoelectronics perform both transmit and receive functions, they are often called transceivers.

Simplified, we can think of the network as being a box, with an electrical signal in one side and an electrical signal out the other side (Figure 2-1).

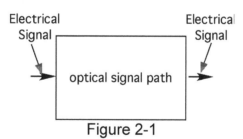

Figure 2-1

When we look in the box, we discover a link, which is the complete optical path between transmitting and receiving devices, or optoelectronics. This path can contain one or more segments. Each segment consists of two fibers in cable[s] and connections. Two fibers are required because data communication systems are full duplex: one fiber carries the transmitted optical signal, the other, the received signal (Figure 2-2).

Connections can be either connectors or splices. Connectors are considered temporary connections because of two capabilities:

1) They can be disconnected to enable replacement of the optoelectronics

2) They can be disconnected to change the routing of the optical signal to a new fiber pair

Splices are considered <u>permanent connections</u>, in that they are rarely disconnected.

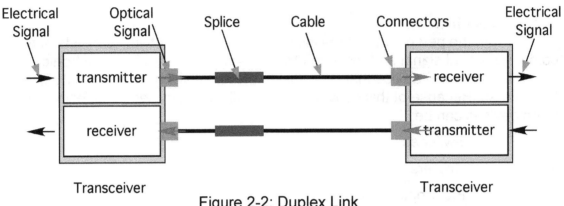

Figure 2-2: Duplex Link

For the purpose of this Guide, we will consider a fiber optic network as a series of links that connect all the optoelectronics. In other words, installers are concerned with links only. More precisely, an installer is concerned with one link at a time.

For the purpose of this Guide, we will use a model link (Figure 2-3). Note that there are three segments in this link: two patch cables and a backbone cable. In many networks, the backbone cable will be a riser cable in a building or a building-to-building backbone cable in a campus.

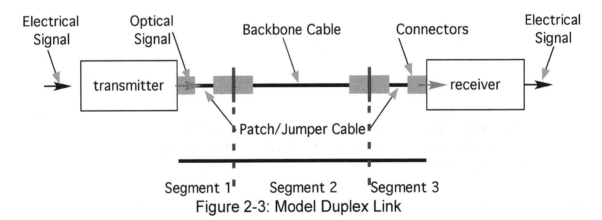

Figure 2-3: Model Duplex Link

3   Light

3.1   Key Terms

Power, link loss, decibels, dB, relative power measurement, OTDR, wavelength, nanometers, nm, speed, optical time domain reflectometer, index of refraction, IR, reflection, refraction, dispersion, skew

3.2   Introduction

The optoelectronics generate or receive an optical signal. The installer needs to understand certain characteristics and behaviors of light in order to be successful.

3.3   Light Characteristics

There are three characteristics that the installer must understand:

Power

Wavelength

Speed

Optical power is important because the link delivers power to the optoelectronics. We all know that all electronic devices must receive a minimum power level in order to operate properly. This fact is true for optoelectronics devices in fiber optic links. The difference is that optoelectronics must receive a minimum optical power level.

If the power loss through the link is excessive, the link will not function properly. Thus, the installer is concerned with link loss. This link loss is measured in units of decibels, or dB, which is a relative power measurement. This loss is the difference between the power delivered to the input end of the link and that at the output end. When the installer measures link loss, current generation optical power meters display this relative power level.

The second characteristic is wavelength. Wavelength is the technical term for the word 'color'. The installer needs to know the wavelength at which the optoelectronics transmit so that he can perform a link loss test at the same wavelength. To do so, he

1) Chooses a testing light source of the same wavelength and

2) Sets the power meter internal calibration to that wavelength

Common wavelengths are 850, 1300, 1310, 1490, and 1550. Wavelengths are measured in nanometers (nm). For more information on how each of these wavelengths is used, see Text Chapters 2 and 3.

The reason the installer must test at the same wavelength as that of the optoelectronics is simple: power loss in optical fibers changes with changing wavelength. For more on this subject, power loss or attenuation, see Text Chapter 3.

The third characteristic is speed of light in the fiber. The installer needs to know this speed in order to calibrate the <u>optical time domain reflectometer</u> or <u>OTDR</u>. This calibration enables the OTDR to display accurate measurements of fiber length and cable attenuation rates.

The OTDR is a test tool that enables the installer to observe the loss through a link. By knowing the loss through a link, the installer can identify and correct locations of high power loss. In addition, an OTDR enables the installer to locate fiber breaks.

The speed of light, in m/sec or miles/hour, is an unwieldy number. To produce a number that is convenient to use, fiber manufacturers provide this speed in the form of the <u>index of refraction (IR)</u>, also known as the refractive index (RI).

The index of refraction is a measure of the speed of light in the fiber. The IR is defined as the ratio of the speed of light in a vacuum to that in the optical fiber. By that definition, the IR is always greater than 1.

For communication optical fibers, the IR varies between 1.4600 and 1.5200. Appendix 1 in the Text provides a list of 60 commonly used indices of refraction.

There are three additional characteristics of light:

Pulse width

Spectral width

Volume

Knowledge of these subtle characteristics becomes important in setting up an OTDR, evaluating light sources, and properly testing singlemode fiber. Such information appears in Text Chapter 2.

3.4   Light Behavior

As light travels through optical fibers and connections, it exhibits certain behaviors. These behaviors are:

Reflection

Refraction

Dispersion

Skew

<u>Reflection</u> occurs in some fibers and at some connections. In fibers, reflection occurs internal to the fiber so that the light travels along the fiber with

minimum 'leakage' or power loss. Such reflection is detailed in Text Chapters 2 and 3.

Reflection occurs in some connections. If this reflection is excessive, the received signal can be different from the transmitted signal. In other words, excessive reflection results in inaccurate signal transmission, which, in turn, will cause the link to fail. With proper installation of connectors and splices, the installer limits such reflection to values that result in accurate signal transmission. See Text Chapters 2, 5, 15, and 16 for more information on reflection, its effects, control thereof, testing thereof, and method of achieving low reflections at connectors.

Refraction, or bending of light, occurs in one type of fiber, known as graded index multimode fiber. This is the type of fiber used in data and video communication links within limited distances, such as buildings, ships, and field-tactical military links. Limited distance can be defined as up to 2000 m.

Dispersion refers to the fact that optical power that enters one end of link at the same time does not exit the other end at the same time. Excessive dispersion can cause a link to fail. As a practical matter, the installer cannot make errors that increase dispersion. However, the installer may need to understand dispersion to troubleshoot malfunctioning links. Dispersion is detailed in Text Chapters 2, 3, and 17.

Skew is of concern in the extremely high data rate links. Such data rates are 40 Gbps and 100 Gbps. To achieve such speeds, the link optoelectronics de-multiplex the signals into parallel signals of 10 Gbps. With de-multiplexing, we require multiple, parallel fibers to carry the signals. 40 Gbps links require 4 transmit and 4 receive fibers; 100 Gbps require 10 transmit and 10 receive fibers. With a little thought, the installer will realize that the parallel signals should arrive at the output end at approximately the same time. The difference in time of arrival between the de-multiplexed signals on different fibers is skew. At this time, skew does not seem to be a problem for installers.

3.5   Other Terms

Spectral width, peak wavelength, central wavelength, critical angle, numerical angle, critical angle, cone of acceptance, NA, NA mismatch

4 Fiber

4.1 Terms

Core, cladding, primary coating, microns (μ), numerical aperture, NA, glass, 8.4μ, 50μ, 62.5μ, 125μ, multimode, step index, graded index, singlemode, maximum attenuation rate, dB/km, typical attenuation rate, Raleigh scattering

4.2 Introduction

Now that the installer understands the basics of light, we can examine the basics of fibers and the manner in which light moves through the fiber. The function of the fiber is accurate transmission of the optical signal. Accurate transmission occurs when both power loss and dispersion are acceptably low.

4.3 Structure

The fiber achieves accurate transmission through its structure. The fiber has at least two, but usually three, regions:

> The core
>
> The cladding
>
> The primary coating

The <u>core</u> is the central region, within which *most* of the optical power travels. The <u>cladding</u> surrounds the core, confines the power to the core, and increases the fiber diameter to make the fiber sufficiently strong and convenient to handle. The <u>primary coating</u> protects the cladding against mechanical and chemical damage (Figure 4-1).

Fibers used in data, CATV, and telephone networks require such protection, since these fibers have <u>glass</u> cores and claddings. See Text Chapter 3 for information on fiber materials other than glass. All three regions are characterized by their diameters, stated in <u>microns (μ).</u>

A= core= 8.4-62.5 μm

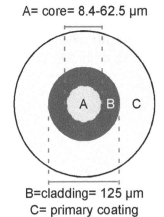

B=cladding= 125 μm
C= primary coating

Figure 4-1: Fiber Structure

Core diameters are <u>8.4μ, 50μ, and 62.5μ</u>, depending on the type and performance of the fiber. For the applications we consider in this Guide, the cladding diameter is always 125 μ. The primary coating is usually 245 μ without color coding and 250 μ with such coding.

A fourth 'dimension' of optical fibers, the numerical aperture (NA), is a measure of the light gathering ability of the fiber. The installer needs to know the fiber NA in order to select test leads for both power loss and OTDR measurements. The NA of the test leads must match the NA of the fibers being tested. Without such matching, loss measurements will be higher than reality. See Text Chapters 2 and 3 for additional NA information.

4.4   Two Basic Fiber Types

There are two basic types of fibers: multimode and singlemode. Multimode fibers have relatively large cores, relatively limited bandwidths, and relatively limited transmission distances. Multimode core diameters are 50 and 62.5 μ.

Bandwidth and transmission distance are related, so no simple bandwidth or distance statement is possible. With that caution, we can state that correctly chosen, multimode fibers can transmit 100 Mbps to 2000 m and 10 Gbps to 550 m.

Multimode fibers have a wide performance range, depending on the structure and diameter of the core. If the core has a single chemical composition, it has limited performance and is not used in communication networks. Such a fiber is called step index.

If the multimode fiber has multiple chemical compositions in the core, up to 2500, it has increased bandwidth and transmission distance. Such a fiber is called graded index. The multiple compositions reduce dispersion and increase both bandwidth and transmission distance. For additional information on these two fiber types, see Text Chapter 3.

Core diameter influences bandwidth and transmission distance. As a general rule, fibers with the 50μ core exhibit higher bandwidth and longer transmission distances than do fibers with the 62.5μ core. In fact, the highest Ethernet standards, 10, 40, and 100 Gbps have been created with the preferred use of 50μ fiber.

Singlemode fibers have relatively small cores, relatively high bandwidths, and relatively long transmission distances. Singlemode core diameters are 8.4-10μ. Singlemode fibers can transmit 1000 Mbps to 5000 m and 10 Gbps to 10,000 m. We leave discussion of the differences in the manner in which light travels in these three types of fibers to Text Chapter 3.

Multimode and singlemode fibers use different wavelengths. In data communication applications, multimode fibers carry 850 and 1300 nm wavelengths while singlemode fibers carry 1310 and 1550 nm wavelengths. In fiber to the home (FTTH) networks, singlemode fibers carry an additional 1490 nm wavelength.

4.5   Light Behavior In Fiber

Once light enters the fiber, the light exhibits two behaviors: dispersion and power loss. As the installer cannot make any errors that result in increased dispersion, we leave that subject to the Text Chapter 3. However, installer errors can result in increased power loss.

The main cause of fiber power loss, or attenuation, in a fiber is <u>Raleigh scattering</u> (Text Chapter 3). Such scattering is the main cause of attenuation in a fiber. The performance parameter most important to the installer is the <u>maximum attenuation rate</u>, in <u>dB/km</u>. If the installer installs the cable properly, the measured attenuation rate will be less than the maximum rate. If the installer installs the cable improperly, the measured rate can exceed the maximum rate. In this situation, there may be insufficient optical power at the optoelectronics. In fact, it is safe to say that:

> <u>All cable installation rules are designed to minimize the power loss in the cable</u>

These maximum rates depend on the fiber type, multimode or singlemode, and the wavelength. These maximum rates range from 0.5 to 3.5 dB/km. See Text Chapter 3 for more detailed information.

The installer will need to know the <u>typical attenuation rate</u> in order to certify the link for maximum reliability. We present certification in Text Chapters 3 and 19 and in Section 15 of this Guide.

4.6   Other Terms

Mode field diameter (MFD), modal dispersion, chromatic dispersion, waveguide dispersion, material dispersion, polarization mode dispersion, core offset, cladding non-circularity, diameter tolerances, zero dispersion wavelength, water peak, total internal reflection, pulse spreading, dispersion shifted fiber, non zero, dispersion shifted fiber, non dispersion shifted fiber, WDM, CWDM, DWDM

5   Cable

5.1   Terms
buffer tube, loose buffer tube, tight buffer tube, multiple fiber per tube [MFPT], central buffer tube [CBT], ribbon, premises, distribution, break out, strength members, jacket, rip cord, maximum installation load, water blocking materials

5.2   Function Of Cable
The glass fiber, with a diameter of 125μ, or about 0.005", cannot survive installation and use without protection. The cable is the package that provides such protection.

5.3   Cable Structure
The cable provides this protection through its structure, which can consist of at least five elements. These elements are:

Buffer tubes

Strength members

Water blocking materials

Jacket(s)

Ripcords

While the full discussion of these elements is too extensive for this Rapid Start Guide, we will present the key terms.

5.3.1   Buffer Tube
The first layer of protection placed on the fiber by the cable manufacturer is the buffer tube. There are two types of buffer tubes and, therefore, two basic types of cables. The buffer tubes can be either loose buffer tubes or tight buffer tubes.

In loose buffer tube cables, the inside diameter of the buffer tube is larger than the outside diameter of the fiber. With this relationship, a loose buffer tube can contain more than one fiber. The common numbers are 12, 6, 216 and over 400.

Three loose tube cable designs are commonly used: multiple fiber per tube [MFPT, a Pearson Technologies' designation], with 12 or 6 fibers per buffer tube (Figure 5-1); central buffer tube, with up to 216 fibers in a single, centrally located buffer tube (Figure 5-2); and the ribbon cable, with more than 400 fibers in a single, centrally located buffer tube (Figure 5-3). Loose tube cables are usually, but not always, used in outdoor networks.

In tight buffer tube cables, the inside diameter of the buffer tube is exactly the same as the outside diameter of the fiber. With this relationship, a tight buffer tube contains only one fiber. Tight tube cables are usually, but not always, used in indoor networks.

There are two tight tube designs, premises (Figure 5-4), also known as distribution, and break out. The break out design is rarely used.

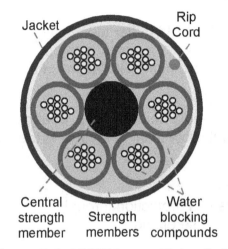

Figure 5-1: MFPT Loose Tube Cable

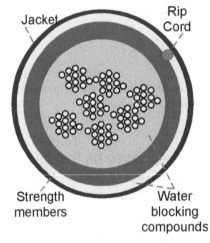

Figure 5-2: Central Buffer Tube Cable

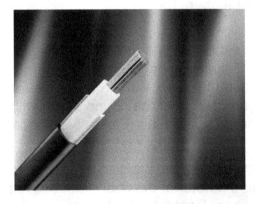

Figure 5-3: Ribbon Cable [Courtesy Corning Cable Systems]

Figure 5-4: Premises Cable

5.3.2   Strength Members

All fiber optic cables contain <u>strength members</u>. During installation, these members restrict elongation of the cable. Excessive elongation can result in fiber breakage. During installation, the installer attaches these strength members to a swivel with a shear pin [Section 10 of this Guide], which, in turn, he attaches to a pull rope.

These strength member materials give the cable its <u>maximum installation load</u> rating. To the installer, installation load rating is one of the three most important performance characteristics of the cable. See Text Chapters 4, 11 and 21 for additional information on cable performance characteristics.

5.3.3   Jacket

All cables have one or more jackets. The jacket protects the inner structure of the cable and is resistant to installation and environmental conditions. For indoor cables, the jacket must comply with the requirements of the National Electrical Code. [NEC]

Removal of the jacket could be a problem, as placement of a knife blade on the jacket might result in damage to the fibers underneath the jacket. The presence of one or more <u>ripcords</u> under the jacket eliminates this potential problem. The ripcord is strong enough that the installer can pull the cord through the jacket, eliminating the need to cut the jacket with a blade.

5.3.4   Other Terms

Water blocking materials, gel and grease blocked, super absorbent polymer, Kevlar, aramid yarn, fiberglass epoxy rods, flexible fiberglass rovings, high strength steel, armor, break out, furcation kit, fan out kit, short term bend radius, long term bend radius, storage temperature range, installation temperature range, operating temperature range, cable colors, vertical rise distance, armor

6   Connectors

6.1   Terms
SC, LC, small form factor, MTP/MPO, ferrule, ceramic, liquid crystal polymer, barrel, installation method, epoxy, hot melt, quick cure adhesive, cleave and crimp, pigtails, 0.75 dB/pair

6.2   Key Aspects
There are four key aspects of fiber optic connectors. They are:

> Type
>
> Ferrule
>
> Loss
>
> Installation method

6.2.1   Type
Although there are at least 19 types of connectors, three are most commonly used today. The author expects that these three will be commonly used in the future. These types are:

> SC
>
> LC
>
> MTP/MPO

Initially offered in the US in 1988, the SC connector is a well-developed, moderate typical loss (0.3 dB/pair), and reliable connector (Figure 6-1). Its use is allowed by TIA/EIA-568-C. Its main disadvantage, large size is expected to result in reduced market share in the future. The SC can be field installed.

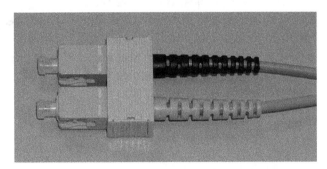

Figure 6-1: Duplex SC Connector

Introduced in the late 1990s, the LC connector is a small form factor (SFF) connector (Figure 6-2). A SFF connector has a size approximately half that of the SC and other pre-SFF connectors. In addition, the LC has the characteristics of low typical loss (0.15-0.20 dB /pair), high reliability, and common use. The author expects the LC to have a large market share in the future.

At time it was first offered, the LC had a unique ferrule: a 1.25 mm diameter, which is half the diameter of the ferrule of the SC connector. Finally, the author has been highly impressed with the performance and reliability of the LC. The LC can be field installed.

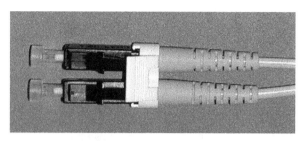

Figure 6-2: Duplex LC Connector

The MTP/MPO is a 12-fiber, ribbon connector (Figure 6-3). It is slightly larger than the SC, yet contains 12 fibers. 40 and 100 Gbps networks will incorporate this connector, because its use reduces rack space consumption. By its design, the MTP/MPO will be factory installed.

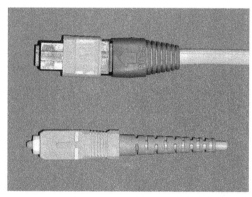

Figure 6-3: 12-Fiber MTP/MPO (top) and 1-fiber SC/APC (bottom)

6.2.2   Ferrule

The ferrule is the tip, or the nose of the connector (Figure 6-4). The ferrule determines the loss of the connector through sub micron alignment of cores.

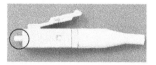

Figure 6-4: Simplex LC Ferrule

Two ferrule materials are commonly used: ceramic and liquid crystal polymer. Ceramic ferrules dominate, though are required only for singlemode connectors. The ceramic is zirconia.

Liquid crystal polymer (LCP) ferrule connectors have reduced cost and the same loss as multimode ceramic ferrules connectors. LCP ferrules have an advantage over ceramic ferrules: they can be re-polished easily to restore original low loss. Repolishing of ceramic ferrules is not always easy or possible.

6.2.3 Loss

The most important connector performance, loss, is rated in dB/pair. A <u>barrel</u> connects two connector plugs to create a pair (Figure 6-5). Today, all data communication connectors are rated at a maximum loss of <u>0.75 dB/pair</u>. When the performance concern is maximum loss, all data communication connectors are the same.

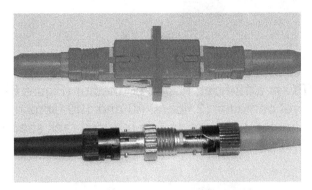

Figure 6-5:" SC And ST-™ Compatible Plugs In Barrels

However, when the performance concern is typical loss, there are differences. Differences result from difference in both the method of installation and the ferrule diameter. Connectors with an installation method that includes polishing and a 2.5 mm ferrule have a typical loss of 0.30 dB/pair. Connectors with an installation method that does not require polishing and a 2.5 mm ferrule have a typical loss of 0.40 dB/pair. Connectors with an installation method that includes polishing and a 1.25 mm ferrule have a typical loss of 0.15-0.20 dB/pair.

6.2.4 Installation Method

There are at least five installation methods used in the US. Four commonly used methods are:

1) Epoxy and polish

2) Hot melt adhesive and polish

3) Quick cure adhesive and polish

4) Cleave and crimp

<u>Epoxy</u> installation requires a two-part epoxy and polishing. Epoxy installation tends to be used in cable assembly facilities. This method allows use of low cost connectors, but has a high labor cost, in man-hours per connector.

<u>Hot melt</u> adhesive connector installation requires connectors that are preloaded with hot melt adhesive and polished. This adhesive needs preheating. The hot melt connector is more expensive than the epoxy connector. However,

the labor cost, in man-hours per connector, is lower than that of epoxy connectors. For field installations, the hot melt connector can provide a total installed cost lower than that of the epoxy connector. Another advantage of this method is the potential for 100 % yield. Installers can achieve 100 % yield through reheating and re-polishing. None of the other three methods offers this same potential. In Pearson Technologies Inc. field installations, we achieve 100 % yield frequently.

The quick cure adhesive method requires a two part 'anaerobic like' adhesive and polishing. This method allows use of low cost connectors. In some cases, this method has low labor cost, in man-hours per connector. However, the process yield for this method can be significantly lower than that of either the epoxy or hot melt methods. As a result, a total installed cost analysis may not favor this method. Finally, this method can have reliability that is less than that of the first two methods. This method is used in field installation and in some cable assembly facilities.

The cleave-and-crimp method requires no epoxy or adhesive and use of a connector with a fiber stub installed by the connector manufacturer. This method requires no polishing. The manufacturer polishes the outside end of the fiber. The manufacturer cleaves the inside end to create a smooth and perpendicular end. The installer cleaves his fiber, inserts it into the connector so that it butts against the installed fiber stub, and crimps the connector to the fiber.

This method requires the highest cost connector, has the lowest labor cost, in man-hours per connector, and requires the lowest amount of training. A total installed cost analysis may, or may not, justify choice of this method.

A little known fact is that fusion splicing of pigtails is the lowest cost method for connector installation. In other words, the lowest cost method of installing connectors is to not install them. A Pearson Technologies' total installed cost analysis has shown that the reduced cost of splicing pigtails can pay for the splicer between 725 and 2200 connectors [http://www.ptnowire.com/tpp-V3-I2.htm].

6.3   Other Terms
ST-™ compatible, back shell, retaining ring, inner housing, outer housing, stainless steel, repeatability, range, contact, non-contact, APC, reflectance, connector colors

See Text Chapters 5, 12, 22-25 for more information on connectors and installation.

7   Splices

7.1   Terms:
Fusion, mechanical, stripping, cleaving, cleaver, active alignment, passive alignment, dressing, index matching gel, reflectance, splice cover

7.2 Splicing Process

Splicing is the process of precision alignment of two fiber ends and fixing those ends in position. All splicing has common features. The splice installer prepares the fiber ends by stripping, cleaning and cleaving. Stripping is removing the primary coating.

Cleaving is the process of creating nearly perfectly perpendicular and smooth ends on both fibers. Cleaving is done with a precision cleaver (Figures 7-1 and 7-2). Precision cleavers produce typical end face angles of 0.5°. Most angles will be less than 1.5°. Cheap cleavers [<$1000] produce cleave angles higher than those produced by moderately priced cleavers [~$1300]. Moderately priced cleavers tend to pay for themselves through reduced time and rework.

Figure 7-1: Cleaver Open For Use

Figure 7-2: Cleaver With Fiber

Since low loss splices require a low cleave angle, a moderate cost precision cleaver is necessary. After cleaving, the process depends on the type of splicing. There are two types of splicing, fusion and mechanical.

7.2.1 Fusion Splicing

Fusion splicing is the process of aligning and fusing, melting, or welding two fibers together. Fusion splicing machines have low [<$10,000] to moderate [$10,000-$15,000] cost (Figures 7-3 and 7-4).

Figure 7-3: Moderate Cost,   Figure 7-4: Alignment Mechanism Of

Active Alignment Splicer   Active Alignment Splicer

Low cost splicing machines use passive alignment of fibers. Passive alignment provides low loss [≤0.10 dB] in two situations. These situations are:

> 1] Splicing of the precise fibers available in North America and in most of the industrialized world

> 2] Splicing of fibers of the same type or from the same fiber manufacturer

Moderate cost splicing machines use active alignment to produce loss of less than 0.05-0.08 dB. This range is less than the values obtained with passive alignment machines. Active alignment machines adjust the positions of the two fibers to achieve the lowest possible loss, even if the fibers have different core or cladding diameters or core offset.

With both passive and active splicing machines, the machine does most of the work, making splicing faster and easier than connector installation. After splicing the fibers, the installer protects the splice by placing one of two types of cover over the splice (Figure 7-5). During the last two steps, the installer places the splice into a splice tray, and places the tray into an enclosure (Figure 7-6).

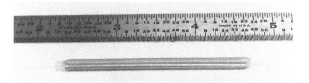

Figure 7-5: Splice Cover

Figure 7-6: Splicer, Splice Tray, and Enclosure

7.2.2   Mechanical Splicing

Mechanical splicing is the process of installing two prepared fiber ends into a mechanical splice (Figure 7-7). The mechanical splice provides two functions: alignment and protection.

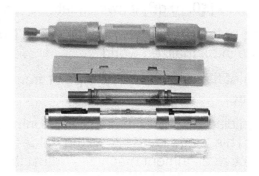

Figure 7-7: Mechanical Splices

All mechanical splices contain an index matching gel. This gel fills any gaps between the fiber ends. Gaps result from cleave angles that are not zero.

This IR of the gel closely matches the index of refraction of the fibers. With this matching, the gel produces low loss [≤ 0.10 dB] and low reflectance. See Text Chapters 2, 5, and 6 for details on reflectance.

Finally, the installer places the splice into a splice tray, and places the tray into an enclosure (Figure 7-6).

7.3   Enclosure Dressing

The process of placing the splice into an enclosure and closing the enclosure is known as dressing. Dressing takes more time than splicing. As

Figure 7-6 demonstrates, the splice has excess fiber, which the installer must coil into the splice tray without breaking or bending the fiber. Bending the fiber can result in excess power loss.

The trays have excess buffer tube that the installer must coil in the enclosure without kinking the tubes. Kinking can result in excess power loss and fiber breakage.

Once the fiber, trays and tubes are in the enclosure, the installer will assemble the enclosure so that it is air and moisture tight. Most of the time spent splicing is spent in actions other than splicing. The precision cleaver, the splicer, and the mechanical splice make achievement of low loss fast and easy. Dressing is not difficult, but is time consuming.

7.4   Other Terms

Splice tray, splice enclosure, splice cover oven, adhesive splice cover, heat shrink splice cover, PAL, LID, V-groove, scribing blade, breaking arm, ribbon splicer

8   Optoelectronics

8.1   Terms
Wavelength, OPBA

8.1.1   Wavelength
From the installer's perspective, only two characteristics of the optoelectronics are important: the wavelength at which the optoelectronics operate and the OPBA. The installer needs to know the <u>wavelength</u> in order to set the light source and power meter to that wavelength. Otherwise, the loss measurements will be meaningless, since they will not simulate optoelectronics operation.

8.1.2   OPBA
The installer needs to know the <u>OPBA</u> rating the optoelectronics. The OPBA is the <u>optical power budget available</u>. It is the maximum power loss that can occur between a transmitter and a receiver while functioning at the specified accuracy level. In other words, as long as the link has a power loss less than or equal to the OPBA, the link will work. Note that the link will work *even if it has been improperly installed.*

8.2   Other Terms
LED, laser diode, VCSEL, minimum required loss, sensitivity, overloading

See Text Chapter 8 for additional information.

9   Cable Installation

9.1   Terms
Installation load, long term bend radius, short-term bend radius, shear pin swivels, slip clutch equipment, load gage equipment, pulleys

9.2   Introduction
During fiber optic link installation, cable installation is the first of two steps at which most problems, cost increases, and power loss increases occur. These problems, etc. occur because the steps for cable installation are subtle and must be followed for the entire process of installing each cable. Overlooking one of these steps can result in obvious high loss, broken fibers, or subtlety reduced reliability. In this section, we present an overview of these steps.

9.3   Two Basic Concerns
There are two concerns that dominate the cable installation process: limiting tensile load applied to the cable and controlling the radius to which the cable is bent.

9.3.1   Installation Load
When a cable is pulled into its location, cable strength members limit the elongation imposed on the fibers. These members are chosen with an assumption of a maximum load applied to the cable. Thus, the installer needs to know this maximum.

TIA/EIA-568-C establishes common <u>maximum installation load</u> values for some cables. These common values are:

Inside plant cable with >12 fibers, 600 lbs-f (2670 N)

Inside plant cable with ≤12 fibers, 300 lbs-f (1335 N)

Outside plant cable, 600 lbs-f (2670 N)

While these values are common, the installer is well advised to determine the actual value from a cable data sheet.

9.3.2   Bend Radii
All cables have two bend radii, below which they cannot be bent without the risk of both increased power loss and fiber breakage. The first bend radius is the <u>short term, or installation, bend radius</u>. This is the minimum radius to which the cable can be bent while under the maximum installation load. This radius is critical when pulling cables into conduit systems in which the direction of the cable changes. Such change occurs in manholes commonly.

TIA/EIA-568-C establishes common short-term minimum bend radius values for some cables. These common values are:

Inside cables with 2-4 fibers: 50 mm at 50 lbs-f (220 N)

Inside cables with ≥4 fibers: 20 times cable outer diameter [OD]

Outside plant cable, 20 times cable OD

The second bend radius is the long term, or unloaded, bend radius. This is the minimum radius to which the cable can be bent while under no load. The cable path imposes this radius on the cable.

TIA/EIA-568-C establishes common long-term minimum bend radius values for some cables. These common values are:

Inside cables with 2-4 fibers: 25 mm

Inside cables with ≥4 fibers: 10 times cable outer diameter [OD]

Inside/outside and outside plant cable, 10 times cable OD

Once again, the installer is well advised to determine the actual bend radius values from a cable data sheet.

9.4   Process
The installer installs the cable in a manner that limits the load applied to the cable and controls the bend radius. While this sounds simple, 'the devil is in the details'.

There are three methods of limiting load: shear pin swivels, slip clutch pulling equipment, and load gage equipment. See Section 10 of this Guide and Text Chapter 11 for details. Such equipment limits the load during the pulling process.

Limiting the installation bend radius requires pulleys or sheaves to control the bend radius at any change in direction. These pulleys must fit in the location at which the direction changes. Manholes can pose problems, because the diameter of the pulley required by the diameter of the cable may be larger than the manhole opening.

Limiting the long-term bend radius is a matter of discipline during installation. Placing a cable in a cable tray, cable trough, enclosure, or raceway requires the installer to remember bend radius control for every second of the installation. A consequence of this need is the ability to see every inch of cable. In addition, forgetting the need for this control for one second can result in excess power loss and fiber breakage.

9.5   Other Terms
NEC compliance, cable lubricants

10   Cable End Preparation

10.1 Terms

Enclosure, shear pin swivel, fan out kit, furcation, dry fiber lubricant

10.1.1   Enclosure

The installer performs cable end preparation twice: once to attach a pull rope to install the cable into its location; and a second time to place the end of the cable into an enclosure (See Text Chapters 11 and 15).

To attach a pull rope to the cable, the installer removes the external jacketing materials to expose the strength members. He removes buffer tubes to avoid applying stress to the fibers. The installer attaches the strength members to a <u>shear pin swivel</u> (Figure 10-1). The shear pin in the swivel has a rating close to but less than the installation load rating. The installer attaches the shear pin swivel to a pull rope. For these actions, the swivel determines the length of strength member to be exposed and the length of jacket to be removed.

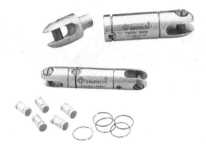

Figure 10-1: Shear Pin Swivel (Courtesy Greenlee-Textron)

An <u>enclosure</u> is a 'box' that protects the end of the cable. This enclosure can be an outdoor splice enclosure (Figure 10-2) or an indoor rack mounted (Figure 10-3) or wall mounted enclosure (Figure 10-4).

Figure 10-2: Outdoor Enclosure

Figure 10-3: Wall Mounted Indoor Enclosure With Pigtail Splices And Integral Patch Panel

Figure 10-4: Rack Mounted Enclosures [Courtesy Panduit Corporation]

To prepare a cable end for installation into an enclosure, the installer must read the instruction sheet for the enclosure into which the end will be placed. This sheet will define the following dimensions:

1) The length of jacket to remove

2) The length of strength member to leave

3) The length of buffer tube to leave

4) The length of fiber with primary coating to expose beyond the end of the buffer tube

If the installer plans to install a fan out kit on fibers from a loose tube cable (Figure 10-5 and Text Chapter 4), the fan out kit instructions may modify these dimensions. In addition, the installer will apply dry fiber lubricant to the fibers so that they slide easily into the fan out tubes. The generic term for fan out is furcation. At this stage, the fibers are ready for either splicing or connector installation.

Figure 10-5: Fan Out Kit

11 Connector Installation

11.1 Terms
Polish, isopropyl alcohol, boot, polishing film, polishing pad, polishing fixture, polishing tool, polishing puck, bead, scriber, lens grade and lint free tissue, air polish

11.2 Assumption
For the purpose of this Guide, we assume that the installer is installing connectors on a tight tube cable or onto 900µ fan out tubing. For installation of connectors onto patch cords, the installer will install and crimp sleeves.

11.3 Introduction
During fiber optic link installation, connector installation is the second of the two steps at which most problems, cost increases, and power loss increases occur. More precisely, most problems occur in polishing.

These problems, etc. occur because the steps for connector installation are subtle and must be followed for each connector. Overlooking one of the steps can result in obvious high loss or subtle reduced reliability. In this section, we present an overview of these steps.

11.4 Common Steps

Regardless of the method of installation, the installer will perform four common steps.

1) Orient and slide a <u>boot</u> onto the buffer tube

2) Strip a specified length of buffer tube and primary coating from the fiber (Length will be specified in connector installation instructions)

3) Clean the fiber with 98 % <u>isopropyl alcohol</u> (or an equivalent cleaner that leaves no residual film) and <u>lens grade, lint free tissue</u>

4) Inspect the fiber to ensure that there are no particles visible on the fiber

The steps that follow depend on the method of installation.

11.5 Method Specific Steps

11.5.1   Epoxy Installation (Text Chapter 22)
Epoxy installation requires the following nine steps.

1) Turn on and set oven to temperature required by epoxy

2) Mix the epoxy thoroughly

3) Transfer epoxy to syringe

4) Inject the proper amount of epoxy into the connector

5) Without bending or breaking the fiber, feed it into the back shell of the connector until the fiber is fully inserted

6) If possible, slide boot over back shell of connector

7) Insert connector into epoxy curing oven for time determined by epoxy

8) Remove connector from oven and allow to cool

9) Polish end

11.5.2 Hot Melt Installation (Text Chapter 24)

1) Install connector into holder

2) Insert holder into oven for specified time

3) Remove holder from oven and insert fiber into connector until it is fully inserted and protrudes beyond end of ferrule

4) Place holder in cooling stand until cool enough to handle

5) Polish end

11.5.3 Polishing

1) Scribe fiber with scriber at tip of bead

2) Pull off excess fiber without bending fiber

3) With 12µ film, polish fiber end so that it is flush with bead of epoxy or adhesive [This is an air polish]

4) Clean end of connector, polishing fixture, polishing pad, and first film

5) Place first film and fixture on polishing pad

6) Insert connector into fixture

7) With light or no pressure, polish in figure 8 pattern until there is no bead (Caution: do not over polish)

8) Clean connector, fixture and second film

9) With pressure, polish in figure 8 pattern for a specified number of figure 8's (level of pressure will be specified in the connector installation instructions)

10) Clean connector, fixture and third film (Third film may not be required for some multimode connectors)

11) With pressure, polish in figure 8 pattern for a specified number of figure 8's (level of pressure will be specified in the connector installation instructions)

12) Clean connector with isopropyl alcohol and lens grade tissues

13) Install boot

14) Place cap on ferrule

11.5.4 Cleave And Crimp (Text Chapter 25)

1) Place connector into connector installation tool

2) Cleave fiber to specified cleave length

3) Insert fiber into connector until fiber butts against pre-installed fiber stub

4) Close and/or crimp connector to fiber and buffer tube

5) Install boot

No polishing is required.

12   Connector Inspection

12.1 Terms
Microscope, visual fault locator (VFL), round, clear, featureless, flush core, clean cladding, clean ferrule

12.2 Inspection Tools
The installer can perform connector inspection with two tools: a microscope and a visual fault locator (VFL). The installer uses a microscope for connectors that require polishing. The installer will use a VFL for connectors that require no polishing.

12.2.1   Microscopic Inspection
The loss of a connector that requires polishing correlates with the appearance of the end of the fiber. In other words, if the connector looks 'good' under the microscope, the connector will test 'good'. If the connectors on both ends of the link look good, the link will test 'good' most of the time. Most means 95 %.

A 'good' connector appearance is defined by 11 words: a good connector has a round, clear, featureless, flush core, a clean cladding and a clean ferrule (Figure 12-1).

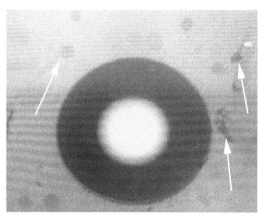

Figure 12-1: A Good Connector With Backlighting

12.2.2   VFL Inspection
For connectors that do not require polishing, the appearance of the end of the fiber will always be good. However, the condition of the fiber ends inside the connector is unknown. It is this condition that determines the loss of the connector.

A visual fault locator is a high power, visible red laser with an adapter that fits the ferrule of the connector. When you insert a connector into the VFL, defect conditions inside the connector will cause the connector to glow. Such conditions can be a bad cleave, dirt on the fiber end, and fiber incompletely inserted into the connector.

The key to VFL inspection is examination the connector on the end of the link opposite to the end that is in the VFL. The end near the VFL will almost always glow, as the VFL launches light into the core and the cladding. Loss of cladding light will occur at the near end. Loss of cladding light will not necessarily indicate a bad connector. Cladding light appears to be lost at the end of the link opposite to the end with the VFL. As it is not present, it will not give a false bad indication.

12.3 Other Terms
Backlighting, magnification

13   Testing- Insertion Loss

13.1 Terms

One lead method, single lead method, Method B, test lead, reference lead, mandrel, power meter, light source, adapter, Category 1, offset control, zeroing control

13.2 Multimode Testing By Method B

There are at least three methods for testing insertion loss of links. However, TIA/EIA-568-C requires that testing of multimode links be performed according to Method B.

Method B requires that the insertion loss be measured with two qualified test leads. The test leads are also known as reference leads.

Method B requires that the input power level be measured with a single test lead. Hence, the alternative name is a 'one lead reference'. To perform a Method B test, the installer performs the following 12 steps.

1. Choose two test leads with same core diameter, NA, and connector type as those under test

2. Qualify reference leads as low loss reference leads

3. Wrap one qualified reference lead around the mandrel suitable for the core diameter and the diameter of the test leads

4. Plug this lead into Category 1 light source and power meter

5. Set source and meter to wavelength at which optoelectronics on link operate

6. Turn on source and meter. Allow reading, in dB, to stabilize.

7. Set meter to 0 dB with offset or zeroing control (Figure 13-1)

8. Disconnect lead from meter. Connect this lead to one end of link.

9. Connect a second reference lead to the meter

10. Connect the other end of the second reference lead to the other end of the link (Figure 13-2)

11. The meter reading is the loss of the link

12. Determine whether measured loss is acceptable. See Section 15 of this Quick Start Guide [Text Chapter 14].

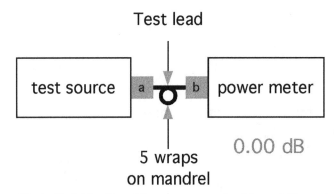

Figure 13-1: Set Up For Measurement of Input Power Level

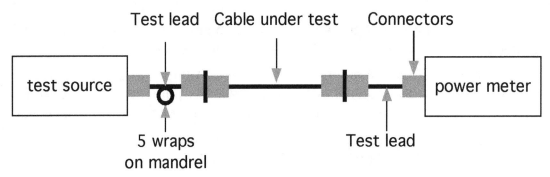

Figure 13-2: Set Up For Measurement of Output Power Level

13.3 SinglemodeTesting

With one exception, the installer performs singlemode testing as described in 13.2 and Figures 13-1 and 13-2. The one exception is the mandrel. For singlemode testing, the installer replaces the mandrel with a single loop with a diameter of 1.2". This loop removes optical power than can be in the cladding.

13.4 Other Terms

Stabilized source, calibrated power meter, directional effects, range, qualified test leads, Method A, modified Method B

14   Testing- OTDR

14.1 Terms

Backscatter coefficient, launch cable, dead zone, blind zone, pulse width, trace, reflective connections, non-reflective connections, multiple reflections, and ghosts

14.2 Method

The installer seta up the OTDR input data. The installer inputs data, which includes wavelength, pulse width, maximum length of cable to be tested, index of refraction of fiber to be tested, maximum time for test or the number of pulses to be analyzed by the OTDR, and backscatter coefficient.

The installer attaches a launch cable to the OTDR. Some manufacturers call this a pulse suppressor, although this cable does not suppress the pulse with current generation OTDRs.

This launch cable should be 3-4 times longer than the dead, or blind zone, of the OTDR. This statement is opinion. In addition, if the maximum length of cables to be tested is under 1 km, you can use a launch cable 10-20 % longer that the longest length. This statement is opinion. Use of a launch cable with these lengths simplifies interpretation by moving multiple reflections, also known as ghosts, to beyond the end of the trace.

The installer plugs the cable to be tested into the end of the launch cable.

The installer runs the OTDR.

When the OTDR has finished, it will display a trace (Figure 14-1). This trace indicates fiber by a straight-line slope, reflective connections by a reflection, or peak, and non-reflective connections by a drop without a peak (Figure 14-2).

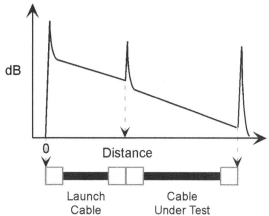

Figure 14-1: OTDR Trace Of Single Segment With Launch Cable

The slopes of the straight-line sections are the attenuation rates of the sections.

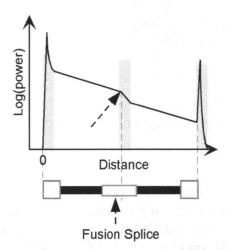

Figure 14-2: OTDR Trace With Non-Reflective Connection

The installer determines the losses in one of two ways.

1] He allows the automatic trace software to determine the loss values

2] He positions cursers on the trace to make loss measurements

The installer compares the measured values to the acceptance values [Section 15 of this Guide].

14.3 Other Terms

Directional differences, gainers, directional bias, average loss in both directions

15   Certification

15.1 Terms

Acceptance values, mid point value

15.2 Definition

The certification process is one of calculating the maximum loss values on an installed link that the installer will accept. The installer determines such values for both the insertion loss and OTDR tests. We will call such values acceptance values.

15.3 Possible Strategies

There are at least three strategies for calculating acceptance values: use of the maximum loss values; use of typical loss values; and use of mid point acceptances values.

15.3.1   Maximum Loss Strategy

One possible strategy is the maximum loss strategy. With this strategy, the installer calculates acceptance values based on the maximum losses of fiber, connectors, and splices. This is the strategy in TIA/EIA-568-C.

The disadvantage with the maximum loss strategy is the fact that:

> Products tend to have loss values closer to the typical value than the maximum value.

Since this is the case, we must ask the question: how can products that perform closer to the typical value than to the maximum value exhibit loss closer to the maximum value than the typical value? Almost always, the answer is: such products have been installed incorrectly.

Examples of incorrectly installed cables are violations of: the bend radii crush load, temperature operating range, vertical rise distance, etc. Examples of incorrectly installed connectors are: cores with damage and contamination on the core, cladding, or ferrule surface. No polish connectors can be installed with dirt on the cleaved fiber, incomplete insertion of the fiber into the connector, or with bad cleaves. Splices can be installed with fibers twisted in enclosures, fiber spiraled inside splice covers, and bend radius violations.

If loss values close to the maximum loss represent installation errors, then it follows that such errors must reduce the reliability of the link. A detailed analysis of such errors supports such reduced reliability.

Form this brief analysis, we can see that there is a risk in using the maximum loss values as acceptance values. That risk is reduced reliability.

15.3.2   Typical Loss Strategy

How can we reduce this risk? We know that the products have a typical loss. Perhaps, we can use the typical loss as an acceptance value. But there is risk with this strategy.

We all know that typical performance means the some products perform slightly worse than the typical value and some perform slightly better. If we use the typical value as a maximum acceptance value, the products that have loss slightly higher than typical will be rejected. Such rejection increases cost of the link without any substantial increase in reliability. Obviously, such a strategy will be not useful, although some organizations have used it.

15.3.3   Mid-Point Strategy

If the use of the maximum loss results in reduced reliability and use of the typical loss results in increased cost, how can we determine acceptable maximum acceptance values? The answer is simple: split the difference. Use a value half way between the maximum loss and typical loss. We call this the mid point value. If loss will be closer to the typical value than the maximum value, it will be at or below the mid point value.

15.4 Recommended Strategy

Our recommended strategy is the mid-point strategy. Text Chapter 19 details the calculations of insertion loss and OTDR acceptance values.

Want More Installation Knowledge?
Get your discounted copy of

Professional Fiber Optic Installation- The Essentials For Success

If you want more information, get your copy of Professional Fiber Optic Installation- The Essentials For Success, from which we extracted much of this Guide. This 342-page, field installation and training manual includes the important information that the installer most needs to be consistently successful. This text shows you how to achieve consistent low installation time and cost, low power loss, and high reliability.

Professional Fiber Optic Installation presents information in four parts: essential information and understanding [Chapters 1-9]; principles of installation [Chapters 10-20]; and installation procedures [Chapters 21-26]. From Chapters 1-9, the installer learns the language of fiber optics, the products used, the advantages and disadvantage of these products, the performance characteristics most important to installers, the typical values of those characteristics, and practical information such as color-coding of cables and connectors.

From Chapters 10-20, the installer learns the reasons behind the rules and procedures of installation; overviews of the procedures for installation, testing, and certification. With this information, you learn the potential problems avoided by following the procedures. It is well known that knowledge of the reasons behind any procedure increases the likelihood of successful following of that procedure.

From Chapters 21-26, the installer learns the detailed procedures of installation. These cook book like, step-by-step procedures enable you to: install cables and prepare their ends [Chapter 21]; install connectors by the methods of epoxy, quick cure adhesive, hot melt adhesive, and cleave and crimp [Chapters 22-25]; inspect and rate connectors with a microscope [Chapter 20]; and make fusion, mechanical, and ribbon splices [Chapters 26]. The 137 figures and photographs in Chapters 20-26 enable the installer to be successful by following the procedures exactly.

Professional Fiber Optic Installation enables the installer to pass the Fiber Optic Association [FOA] and ETA certification examinations. In addition, Chapters 11-15 enable passing of the three highest FOA certifications, the Certified Fiber Optic Specialist [CFOS/C, CFOS/S, and CFOS/T].

At least 12 schools have used the previous version of Professional Fiber Optic Installation as a training text. Pearson Technologies Inc. has used versions of this text for training of more than 5586 trainees. These trainees have been from organizations such as: US Army, US Air Force, US Navy, US Coast Guard,

Environmental Protection Agency, Bureau Of Land Management, Verizon, ATT, National Security Agency, Rolls Royce, and NASA.

Not convinced that Professional Fiber Optic Installation will lead you to success? Review the Table of Contents (http://www.ptnowire.com/Sfoi-outline-7.2.htm). From its 342 pages, 526 figures, 27 chapters, 407 review questions, 28 field procedures, 33 training procedures, and 57 tables, you'll be convinced that this text is both comprehensive and practical.

> If you have purchased this Rapid Study Guide, your cost of Professional Fiber Optic Installation- The Essentials For Success is $39, plus USPS shipping of $5. To receive the discounted price, please provide a copy of your purchase confirmation as an email document or a .pdf. Without this purchase, your price is $49, plus $5 USPS shipping.

To order your copy, send us an email requesting your copy. Send the email to fiberguru@ptnowire.com. We will initiate a payment request through PayPal. When we receive confirmation of payment, we will ship your copy of this well received, comprehensive installation manual. Usual shipment is within 4 working days of receipt of confirmation.

www.ingramcontent.com/pod-product-compliance
Lightning Source LLC
Chambersburg PA
CBHW060509060326
40689CB00020B/4692